MONK

(A Fascinating Book Containing Monkey Facts, Trivia, Images & Memory Recall Quiz: Suitable for Adults & Children)

By

Matthew Harper

Image Courtesy of gmad

For legal reasons we are obliged to state the following:

Copyright 2014 Matthew Harper

ISBN-13: 978-1500392253

ISBN-10: 1500392251

All rights reserved. No reproduction, copying or transmission of this publication, CD's or DVD included in this system may be made without written permission. No paragraph of this publication may be reproduced, copied or transmitted without written permission, or in accordance with the Copyright Act 1956 (amended).

Hi and a very warm welcome to "Monkeys". A Fascinating Book Containing Monkey Facts, Trivia, Images & Memory Recall Quiz: Suitable for Adults & Children.

I'm one of those people who loves to hear about extraordinary facts or trivia about anything. They seem to be one of the few things my memory can actually recall. I'm not sure if it's to do with the shock or the "WoW" factor but for some reason my brain seems to store at least some of it for a later date.

I've always been a great believer in that whatever the subject, if a good teacher can inspire you and hold your attention, then you'll learn! Now I'm not a teacher but the system I've used in previous publications on Amazon seems to work well, particularly with children.

This edition includes a selection of those "WoW" facts combined with some pretty awesome pictures, if I say so myself! At the end there is a short "True or False" quiz to check memory recall and to help cement some of the information included in the book. Don't worry though, it's a bit of fun but at the same time, it helps to check your understanding.

Please note that if you're an expert on this subject then you may not find anything new here. If however you enjoy hearing sensational and extraordinary trivia and you like looking at some great pictures then I think you'll love it.

Matt.

In true Matthew Harper tradition, I thought that before we get down to some of those amazing facts, we might begin with a few snapshots, just to get the juices flowing..............

SQUIRREL MONKEY

Image Courtesy of LaertesCTB

SPIDER MONKEY

Image Courtesy of Neil Saunders

HOWLER MONKEY

Image Courtesy of laird.perkins

PATAS MONKEY

Image Courtesy of Eric Kilby

COLOBUS MONKEY

Image Courtesy of Tambako the Jaguar

DRILL MONKEY

Image Courtesy of Dimitry B

DOUC LANGUR MONKEY

Image Courtesy of Dakiny

ROLOWAY MONKEY

Image Courtesy of Glen Bowman

SPECTACLED LANGUR

Image Courtesy of M. Lehmkuhler

GOLDEN LION TAMARIN

Image Courtesy of wwarby

Okay. Hope that helped to get you in the mood.

HERE WE GO..

Image Courtesy of jsstrn

Did you know that the smallest monkey in the world is the Pygmy Marmoset which is found in the Amazon and weighs only 100 grams?

Image Courtesy of Tambako the Jaguar

Did you know that monkeys are classified into Old World monkeys (from Africa and Asia) and New World monkeys (from South America)?

Image Courtesy of torbus

Did you know that Albert II was the name of the first monkey to reach outer space in 1949?

Did you know that, generally speaking, one of the main differences between Monkeys and Apes are that the former have tails whereas the latter have no tails?

Image Courtesy of Eric Kilby

Did you know that when monkeys are signalling aggression they do this by pulling at their lips or by yawning?

Image Courtesy of drew007m

Did you know that there are currently around 260 known species of monkey in the world?

Image Courtesy of mejymejy

Did you know that the tail of a monkey, which can hold or grasp objects, is known as a prehensile tail?

Image Courtesy of marko8904

Did you know that the brain of the monkey is considered a delicacy in south-east Asia and China?

Image Courtesy of miheco

Did you know that the Mayan people of Mexico worshipped the monkey believing they were incarnations of dead ancestors?

Image Courtesy of Wolfgang Sauber

Did you know that a group of monkeys is known either as a troop or a tribe of monkeys?

Image Courtesy of oldandsolo

Did you know that the only species of monkey found in Europe is the Barbary Macaque?

Image Courtesy of DavidDennisPhotos.com

Did you know that the Spider monkey, found in Central and South America, has no thumbs?

Did you know that it was the Rhesus monkey which lent its name to the blood group of the same name?

Image Courtesy of jinterwas

Did you know that the famous Capuchin monkeys of South America are named after a group of friars because the explorers thought they looked similar?

Image Courtesy of Tambako the Jaguar

Did you know that the Howler monkey is so loud that its howls can be heard over 10 miles away?

Image Courtesy of poplinre

Did you know that one of the main ways that monkeys communicate is by altering their facial expressions?

Image Courtesy of seeveeaar

Did you know that the monkey represents the ninth year of the twelve year Chinese calendar and that the next year of the monkey is 2016?

Did you know that grooming plays a large role amongst monkeys as it's considered vital for socializing and bonding?

Image Courtesy of tristanf

Did you know that monkeys don't actually eat banana peel? They throw it away just like humans do.

Image Courtesy of acameronhuff

Did you know that there's a breed of monkey called the Proboscis, so named because of its noticeably large and growing nose?

Image Courtesy of David Dennis

Did you know that the term Haplorrhini is the name that scientists give to the species of monkeys around the world?

Image Courtesy of Marcel Burkhard

Did you know that monkeys play a role in the divine entities of Hinduism given that Hanuman is considered a type of monkey god?

Did you know that the Mandrill is the world's largest monkey and is mostly found in southern Cameroon, Equatorial Guinea and the Congo?

Image Courtesy of Alois Staudacher

Did you know that Old World monkeys from Africa and Asia have trichromatic vision like that of humans?

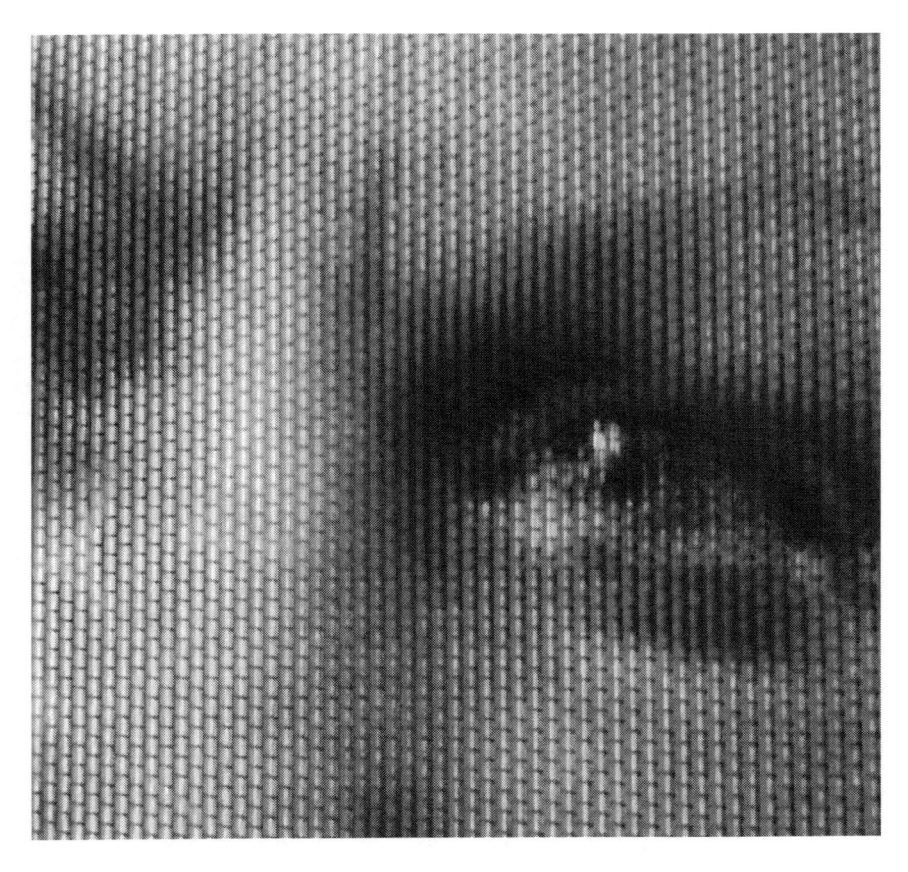

Image Courtesy of Martin Howard

Did you know that many species of monkey, particularly those in south-east Asia, use stone tools to smash oysters and nuts to obtain the food therein?

Image Courtesy of timsnell

Did you know that the average age a monkey can live to is 45 years old?

Image Courtesy of warriorwoman531

Did you know that the average gestation period, depending on the species of monkey, is between 4-8 months long?

Image Courtesy of micsten

Did you know that Old World monkeys have only 32 teeth compared to 36 teeth that the New World monkeys have?

Image Courtesy of Tim simpson1

Did you know that monkeys can breed at any time of the year, just like humans?

Image Courtesy of williamcho

Did you know that monkeys are very susceptible to becoming carriers of serious diseases such as tuberculosis and hepatitis?

Image Courtesy of oldandsolo

Did you know that not all monkeys have long tails? The Stump-Tailed Macaque and the Barbary Macaque for example are often mistaken for apes.

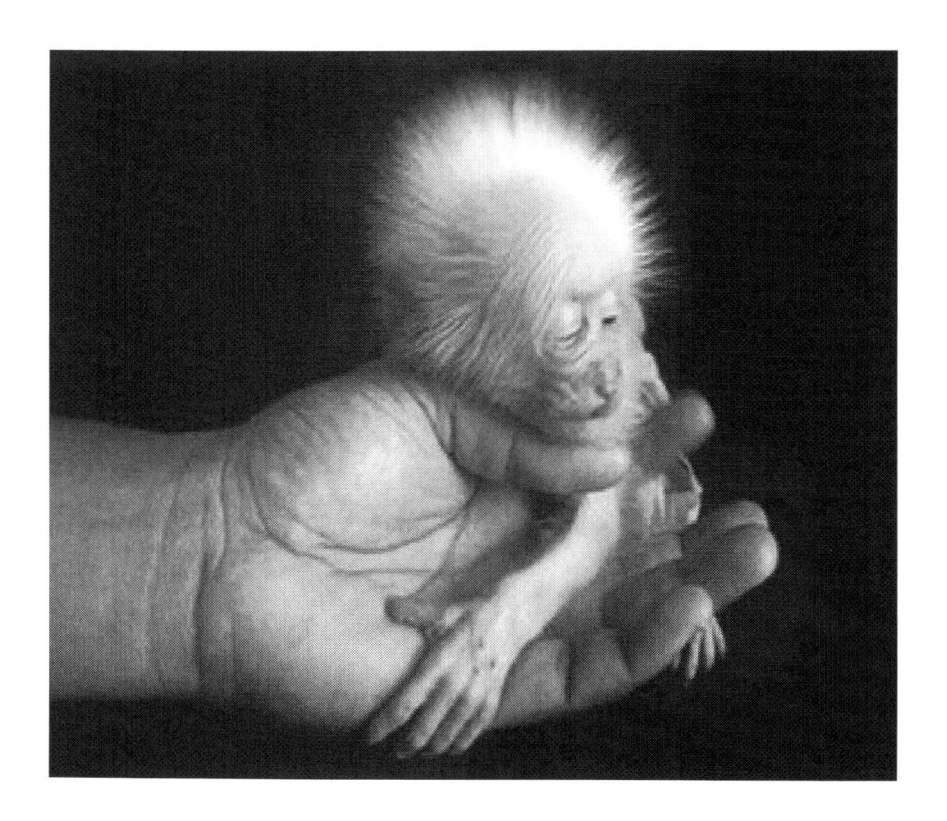

Did you know that the Owl monkey has the largest eyes of any primate in South America? This comes in handy for night vision.

Image Courtesy of GollyGforce - Living My Worst Nightmare

Did you know that the Lemur, has a pointed head and curved nostrils?

Did you know that the tip of a Spider monkey's tail can support its full weight?

Image Courtesy of Michael Schamis

Did you know that most monkeys do not swing arm-to-arm through the trees? They actually run across the branches.

Image Courtesy of jinterwas

Did you know that out of the 141 species of new world monkeys, 33 are classified as endangered?

Image Courtesy of GregPC

Did you know that the Capuchin monkey is widely considered to be the smartest of the New World species?

Image Courtesy of Frans de Waal

Did you know that the South American Titi monkey mates for life?

Image Courtesy of cliff1066

Did you know that between 100,000 and 200,000 non-human primates are believed to be used for scientific research every year?

Image Courtesy of Adhi Rachdian

Did you know that the Black Bearded Saki is the only dark-nosed species of Bearded Saki that has a blackish back? It is listed as critically endangered.

Image Courtesy of Ronbeam2011

Did you know that the White-Cheeked Spider Monkey provides seed dispersal for about 138 different species of fruit seeds all around its habitat?

Images Courtesy of Miguelrangeljr

Did you know that the Guatemalan Black Howler monkey is not only the largest of the Howler species but it's also one of the largest of the New World monkeys?

Image Courtesy of Dave Johnson

Did you know that the Greater Spot-Nosed monkey is one of the smallest Old World monkeys and is native to West Africa? It is also sometimes referred to as the Putty-Nosed monkey.

Image Courtesy of LaetitiaC

Did you know that the Crab-Eating Macaque has a cheek pouch used for storing its food whilst foraging? Interestingly, they do not typically eat crab!

Image Courtesy of John Mauremootoo

Did you know that Chlorocebus monkeys can live in groups comprising up to 76 individuals?

Image Courtesy of oldandsolo

Did you know that Geoffroy's Tamarin spends virtually all its life in the trees?

Image Courtesy of brunkfordbraun

Did you know that the Aegyptopithecus lived over 30 million years ago and closely resembled our modern-day New World monkey?

Image Courtesy of Nobu Tamura

Did you know that the Nilgiri langur lives in the Nilgiri Hills in South India? It also faces extinction due to deforestation and poaching.

Image Courtesy of cprogrammer

Did you know that although Silvered Leaf monkeys are silver to dark grey in colour, their babies are orange?

Image Courtesy of HooLengSiong

Did you know that Olive Colobus monkeys are hunted for food both by humans & chimpanzees?

Image Courtesy of Chi King

That's about it for the trivia for now. I'd like to finish this publication with TEN "True or False" questions based on what you've just read. It should help you to really cement the information and to test your memory recall!

....
....

DON'T FORGET TO KEEP YOUR SCORE: THERE'S 1 POINT FOR EACH OF THE FIRST 9 QUESTIONS AND 5 POINTS FOR THE BONUS QUESTION GIVING A TOTAL OF 14 POINTS ....

1.

TRUE or FALSE: The smallest monkey in the world is the Pygmy Marmoset.

TRUE

2.

TRUE or FALSE: Arthur II was the name of the first monkey to reach outer space in 1949.

FALSE

ALBERT II was the name of the first monkey to reach outer space in 1949.

3.

TRUE or FALSE: A group of monkeys is known either as a troop or a tribe of monkeys.

TRUE

4.

TRUE or FALSE: The Spider monkey, found in Central and South America, has no thumbs.

TRUE

5.

TRUE or FALSE: The Howler monkey is so loud that its howls can be heard over 100 miles away.

FALSE

The Howler monkey is so loud that its howls can be heard over **10** miles away.

6.

TRUE or FALSE: Old World monkeys have only 32 teeth compared to 36 teeth that the New World monkeys have.

TRUE

7.

TRUE or FALSE: The South American Titi monkey mates with many females throughout its life.

FALSE

The South American Titi monkey **MATES FOR LIFE**.

8.

TRUE or FALSE: Chlorocebus monkeys can live in groups comprising up to 76 individuals.

TRUE

9.

TRUE or FALSE: Aegyptopithecus lived over 30 million years ago.

TRUE

10.

BONUS ROUND WORTH 5 POINTS

TRUE or FALSE: The Mandrill is the world's largest monkey.

TRUE

Congratulations, you made it to the end!

I sincerely hope you enjoyed my little monkey project and that you learnt a thing or two. I certainly did when I was doing the research. Very sad that so many monkeys suffer and die in the name of science!

ADD UP YOUR SCORE NOW.

1 point for each of the first 9 correct answers plus 5 points for the bonus round giving a grand total of 14 points.

If you genuinely achieved 14 points then you are indeed a

"MONKEY MASTER".

8 to 13 points proves you are a **"MONKEY LEGEND"**.

4 to 7 points shows you are a **"MONKEY ENTHUSIAST"**.

0 to 3 points shows you are a **"MONKEY ADMIRER"**.

NICE WORK!

Matt.

Thank you once again for choosing this publication. If you enjoyed it then please let me know using the Customer Review Section through Amazon.

If you would like to read more of my work then simply type in my name using the Amazon Search Box and hopefully you'll find something else that "takes your fancy" or go directly to my website printed below.

Until we meet again,

Matthew Harper

www.matthewharper.info

Image Courtesy of gmad